ALEUTIAN ADVENTURE

ALEUTIAN ADVENTURE

KAYAKING IN THE BIRTHPLACE OF THE WINDS

BY JON BOWERMASTER
PHOTOGRAPHS BY BARRY TESSMAN

NATIONAL GEOGRAPHIC SOCIETY

WASHINGTON, D.C.

Published by the National
Geographic Society
1145 17th Street, N.W.
Washington, D.C. 20036-4688

All rights reserved.

Staff for this book

Nancy Laties Feresten
*Publishing Director,
Children's Books*

Suzanne Patrick Fonda
Editor

Annie Griffiths Belt
Illustrations Editor

Marianne Koszorus
Design Director

David M. Seager
Designer

Carl Mehler
Director of Maps

Matt Chwastyk
Gregory Ugiansky
Martin S. Walz
Map Research and Production

Janet Dustin
Illustrations Assistant

Lewis R. Bassford
Production Manager

R. Gary Colbert
Production Director

Vincent P. Ryan
Manufacturing Manager

Text, legends, and headings for days are set in Lubalin Graph; dates and journal entry headings are set in Aachen Bold.

Cover: Sean Farrell fights rain and frigid seas as he paddles his kayak in Alaska's Aleutian Islands.

Half title page: With kayaks loaded, the team heads across British Columbia, in Canada, on their way to Alaska.

Full title page: Carlisle's snow-covered volcano makes a striking landmark for the kayakers.

Dedication page: Journal writing was a daily activity, rain or shine.

Library of Congress Cataloging-in-Publication Data

Bowermaster, Jon 1954-
    Aleutian adventure : kayaking in the birthplace of the winds / by Jon Bowermaster;photographs by Barry Tessman.
        p. cm.
        ISBN 0-7922-7999-9 (hc.)
        1. Sea kayaking–Alaska–Aleutian Islands.
2. Bowermaster, Jon,1954—Journeys–Alaska–Aleutian Islands.
I. Title: Kayaking in the birthplace of the winds. II. Tessman, Barry, ill. III. Title.

GV776.A4 B69 2001
797.1'224'097984–dc21   00-055885

Printed in the U.S.A.

For Brigitte and Victoria
—JB

For Joy and Ellie Rose
—BT

Jon Bowermaster

Barry Tessman

Sean Farrell

Scott McGuire

Introduction

When I was 12 years old, I dreamed about becoming a sports writer. I loved baseball. To me, there was nothing better than going to the ballpark, eating hot dogs, writing up the story of the game, seeing my name in the paper, and then doing it all over again the next day.

As I grew up and began traveling the world, my idea changed a little. Instead of writing about teams and sports, I decided to focus on adventure and remote corners of the world: dogsledding to the North Pole, rafting wild rivers in China, and riding horses through Patagonia in South America.

The combination of writing and adventure is what led me to organize a four-man kayaking trip to the Islands of Four Mountains in the Aleutians, a chain of volcanic islands that stretches across the Bering Sea between Alaska and Russia. We spent five weeks exploring this little-known place – paddling the waters, climbing the volcanoes, and looking for traces of the Aleut people who for thousands of years made this small group of islands their home.

It wasn't easy. The weather conditions in this area are some of the worst in the world. It is famous for fierce winds and thick fog, and the ocean currents and tides are treacherous. The trip was an extreme challenge for our kayaking and survival skills. Coming back alive was our main priority.

The team was a mix of friends, old and new. Photographer Barry Tessman and I have traveled around the world together on a variety of big adventures, from river rafting in China and Chile to sea kayaking in Mexico and Central America. Sean Farrell, a friend of Barry's from college, is a lawyer whose real passion is sailing. His excellent skills with a compass and a Global Positioning System (GPS) – a computer about the size of a portable phone that can tell you where you are within a few feet – were invaluable in navigating through the fog. Scott McGuire, the youngest of our team, sells outdoor gear up and down the West Coast.

He is tall and strong and has spent thousands of hours in sea kayaks.

Because we live on opposite sides of the country – I live in New York; Barry, Sean, and Scott live in California – we did not have a lot of time to train together. We met for one long weekend at Barry's house to test the equipment we'd gathered – everything from kayaks and life jackets to paddles and stoves – and to work on rescue techniques. Our biggest worry was flipping a kayak. Even in summer, the temperature of the Bering Sea is just above freezing; if we ended up in the water, we knew we would have only a few minutes to get back into the boat. Any longer and we could die from hypothermia. It would be impossible to get help in such a short period of time. It would be up to us to save ourselves.

The tiny rectangle on the globe marks the Islands of Four Mountains, the remote region in the Aleutian chain where our kayaking adventure took place. The map shows our route from start to finish.

One of the most difficult parts of an expedition like ours was that we had to bring everything we needed. The nearest supermarket would be in Dutch Harbor, Alaska, more than 150 miles away; the closest shopping mall would be 1,000 miles away. At the outset each kayak was stuffed with about 600 pounds of clothing and gear for paddling and climbing; a tent; two sleeping bags; a cookstove and fuel; breakfast, lunch, and dinner for 35 days; navigation equipment; a radio; flares; and emergency beacons. We doubted these would attract much attention in such a remote area, but we felt safer having them along.

I searched for people who might be able to tell us about these islands but found few who had even seen them. Those who had, described them as "magical." We were sure of one thing: We would be the first since the Aleuts mysteriously left 150 years ago to kayak from island to island and set foot on all five shores. We could only imagine what we would find.

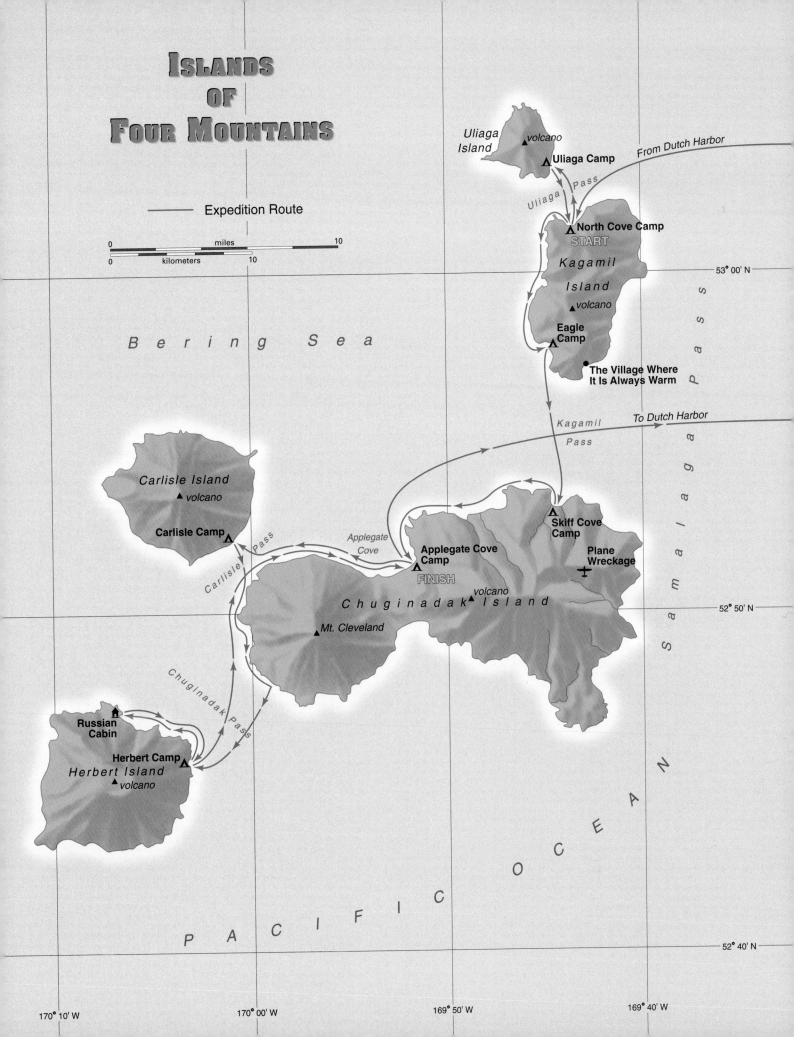

ISLANDS OF FOUR MOUNTAINS

Expedition Route

miles
0   10

kilometers
0   10

Uliaga Island

▲ volcano

Uliaga Camp ⚑

From Dutch Harbor

Uliaga Pass

North Cove Camp ⚑
START

Kagamil Island

▲ volcano

Eagle Camp ⚑

● **The Village Where It Is Always Warm**

B e r i n g   S e a

Kagamil Pass   *To Dutch Harbor*

53° 00' N

Skiff Cove Camp ⚑

Carlisle Island

▲ volcano

Carlisle Camp ⚑

Carlisle Pass

Applegate Cove

Applegate Cove Camp ⚑
FINISH

Plane Wreckage ✈

Chuginadak   Island

▲ volcano

▲ Mt. Cleveland

52° 50' N

Chuginadak Pass

🏠 **Russian Cabin**

Herbert Camp ⚑

Herbert Island

▲ volcano

S a m a l a g a   P a s s

P A C I F I C   O C E A N

52° 40' N

170° 10' W   170° 00' W   169° 50' W   169° 40' W

June 13: On Board the Miss Peppers

The ten-foot-tall, coal black ocean waves are a perfect match for the Alaskan night sky. The fishing boat we are riding in – the *Miss Peppers* – rocks hard each time it plows into a new wave. With every crash the contents of the boat's cabin – donuts, soda cans, maps, Styrofoam cups, rain jackets – go flying. It feels like we are motoring through a hurricane.

It is pouring rain, and the temperature is barely above freezing. All evening, I kept my eye on Captain Don Graves and his assistant Nick as they took turns steering the boat through the rough seas. They have to fight to keep the boat on course. With each crash my three teammates looked at me with wide eyes as if to ask, Are you sure you know what you're getting us into?

We are in the middle of the Aleutian Islands, a chain of more than a hundred small islands, strung like a 1,400-mile-long pearl necklace between the Pacific Ocean and the cold waters of the Bering Sea. The islands take their name from the

When we loaded our gear onto the ferry that would take us to Dutch Harbor, Alaska (right), it was rainy and foggy. It wasn't until we were out on the Bering Sea that the clouds lifted. For the first time we could see the impressive volcanic peaks that dot the Aleutians.

Aleuts, the native people who first populated them as many as 9,000 years ago. We are headed to a group of islands the Aleuts believe is their birthplace: the Islands of Four Mountains. It is also known as the Birthplace of the Winds because of the 100-mile-an-hour winds that often blow there.

It's just after midnight, and I have finally crawled into a bunk in the bow of the boat, hoping to get a couple hours of sleep. Burrowing under a sleeping bag, I brace myself against the pounding waves and listen to the howling wind. I wonder myself, Should we have come?

June 14: First Camp

Early this morning – after 12 hours of crashing through the waves – the *Miss Peppers* pulled into North Cove, a small bay on Kagamil Island. The fog was so thick we could barely see the shoreline. We paddled our kayaks ashore and unloaded our gear as fast as we could. The crew of the *Miss Peppers* was anxious to get back to Dutch Harbor before the weather got any worse.

We struggled in the strong wind to put up our two gray-and-orange tents – the same kind climbers use on Mount Everest. Barry and Sean decided to put their tent on the sandy beach. Scott and I climbed up the grassy cliff and picked a site overlooking the ocean. We secured the tents against the strong winds with lines wrapped around big pieces of driftwood or rocks that we buried deep in the ground. "It won't get any better than this," laughed Barry, as he dragged a big log down the beach. He is probably right. We had picked North Cove as our first camp because of its long, sandy beach.

Our first landing was on the black sand beach of North Cove on Kagamil Island (below). We had crossed the same waters where Aleuts had hunted whales from their kayaks for thousands of years.

Once we leave here we expect to camp mostly on rocks and boulders.

We're quickly developing a good camp routine. Scott and I share one of the two-man kayaks, so we also share a tent and the cooking and cleaning chores that go with it. Same goes for Sean and Barry. We'll keep our clothes and food in our own boats. This should eliminate the problem of trying to remember where we packed our oatmeal or that extra pair of socks.

It has rained steadily today, except for a few periods when strong winds blew the rain and clouds away and gave us a glimpse of Uliaga, the nearest island. Within half an hour the rain and fog always returned. The whistling of the wind and the crashing of the waves are

Most of the beaches in the Aleutians are rocky, so camping on black, volcanic sand was a luxury – and much more comfortable.

the only sounds, except for the occasional chirp of a puffin flying overhead, checking out the new neighbors.

We cooked – and ate – our first meal inside. We set up the small gas stoves near the opening of each tent. The flame is hot but tiny, so there's little risk of catching the tents on fire. Scott filled a water bag with fresh water from a stream running down the hill beside our tent, and we cooked pasta with tomato sauce.

Although the sea around the islands is full of fish, we knew we wouldn't be able to rely on catching any, so we brought all of our food: oatmeal for breakfast; nuts, chocolate, and an energy snack called Gu for lunch; pasta and rice for dinner. If these run out, we have freeze-dried meals we can prepare simply by adding boiling water.

North Cove had one of the few beaches where we found driftwood, which we used to make windbreaks and campfires. It took both Scott and Sean to pull this water-soaked log across the beach. Too wet to burn, it made an excellent bench.

Day 3

June 15: First Crossing

Today we made our first crossing. We knew it wouldn't be easy. Looking at the pass through our binoculars, we saw whitecaps and big waves between Kagamil and Uliaga. The current moved like a powerful, fast-moving river. It required all of our strength and experience to get across safely. Our biggest fear – and the reason none of us had slept particularly well – was of being pushed out to sea, drifting toward Japan or Hawaii thousands of miles away. This first crossing had haunted us all for many months, and we were anxious to get it behind us.

Because of the cold, we dressed in our full paddling suits. Each of us wore a Gore-Tex dry suit, sealed by rubber at the wrists and ankles. Underneath was a thick "bunny suit" made

of Polartec fleece. Rubber hats lined with fleece covered our heads, and we wore two pairs of water-resistant socks under our shoes. Our hands were protected by neoprene (a kind of rubber) gloves. Only our cheeks and noses were exposed to the air.

Unlike some expeditions we don't have a base camp. Every time we kayak we have to pack everything into our boats. We know that storms

Sean shows off his brown "bunny suit" as he thaws his near-frozen feet. Clothing made of Gore-Tex, Polartec fleece, and neoprene made up our full paddling suits (right).

with 100-mile-per-hour winds come up fast out here and can last a week. We could get stuck on another island. Without food or tents, we'd die from exposure. It is smarter and safer to take everything with us each time we head out on the water.

Our kayaks are among the biggest in the world – 22 feet long, with room for two people plus another 500 to 600 pounds of gear. They are the same shape as the kayaks invented and used by the Aleuts. They called their boats *ikyaks*, and they were like ours in many ways. The biggest difference is in the materials used to construct them. Aleut kayaks were built from whalebone and sealskin; ours are made of fiberglass and an ultralight, super-strong material called Kevlar.

When Scott and I pushed our heavily loaded boat off the beach into the surf, we had our first near disaster. The rubber skirt designed to fit over my cockpit is brand new – and stiff. Before I could pull it completely over the opening, a large wave broke over the front of the boat, flooding my lap with 35°F Bering Sea water and half filling my cockpit.

"Start bailing," shouted Scott. As he paddled, I grabbed the pump. I held it with one hand and pushed and pulled the handle with the other until all the cold water was sucked out of the cockpit back into the sea.

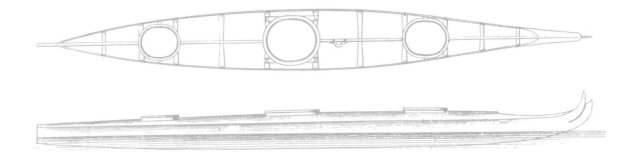

At Eagle Cove we placed our kayaks on "beds" made of buoys that had washed off fishing boats. The buoys helped keep the boats from rubbing against the rocks in big winds. We wondered how the Aleuts kept their skin-covered kayaks (above) from tearing on the rocks.

Cold water. It is our biggest danger. Having my cockpit flood was an instant reminder of just how careful we have to be. If we capsize in these waters, we will have just a few minutes to turn the boat over and crawl back in before our body temperature starts to drop. If we stay in the water more than 10 or 15 minutes, our arms and legs will grow weak. Getting back into the boat – which can be tough even in warm water – will be extremely difficult, if not impossible. We could drown or, if our body temperature dropped below 90°F, die of hypothermia.

My cockpit empty of water, we headed through a thick blanket of fog for Uliaga. It was the first time we had

paddled any distance in nearly a month. I felt rusty and anxious, but within 15 minutes we had settled into a good, steady pace. A strong current tried to push us off course. Paddling harder, we managed to plow through the waves in a straight line toward our goal, which was still hidden from view. An hour later we reached the calm water near Uliaga and breathed a big sigh of relief. We made it! Our first crossing is behind us!

Many of our crossings were done in the fog. It was frightening not being able to see what was around us after leaving land, but fog isn't all bad. It usually means less wind and calmer seas.

Day 4

June 16: Foiled by the Wind

We spent yesterday exploring Uliaga on foot. We hiked 2,000 feet up its volcano, trying to climb above the fog to catch a glimpse of the much bigger volcanoes on Carlisle and Chuginadak. When we returned to North Cove's black sand beach, it felt like home.

Today we planned to paddle about ten miles to the southern end of Kagamil. Instead, we had our first lesson in why this place is nicknamed the Birthplace of the Winds. We took down our camp late in the morning and hoped to start paddling early in the afternoon. That would allow us to take advantage of the outgoing tides. We folded our tents, stuffed sleeping bags into their sacks, put all of the food into waterproof bags, and carried everything down to the shoreline. Just as we finished loading the kayaks, the strongest wind we'd seen kicked up out on the sea. We could see it whipping up "williwaws" – small tornadoes – on the water between Kagamil and Uliaga. It was obvious what we had to do: unpack our boats and set up camp all over again.

"Good call," said Barry, as we struggled to put up our tents in the fierce wind. "It's a good thing we weren't out on the water when this storm arrived."

"You're right. We could have been blown all the way to Kamchatka," joked Sean.

Loading and unloading several hundred pounds of gear from our kayaks was a major part of each day. Each time we paddled, we had to take down our tents, pack up the cook stoves and all our food and clothing, then set everything up again at a new camp.

Day 6

June 18: Puffin Encounter

Uliaga I.

—— Travel
----- Previous Travel
▲ Volcano

North Cove Camp

Kagamil I.

Bering Sea

▲ Eagle Camp

Carlisle I.

N

PACIFIC OCEAN

0 miles 10
0 km. 10

Today was our first peaceful day of paddling. We traded our fleece-lined headgear for baseball caps and headed out of North Cove for a small, rocky beach we'd identified on the map. When we rounded Kagamil's northwest corner and paddled south along the coast, we could see – for the first time – all of Uliaga, beautiful against a bright blue sky.

With the sunshine came hundreds, maybe thousands, of birds. Puffins, murres, ptarmigans, gulls, and eagles flew out to inspect us. The birds nest in the rocks along the steep, rocky cliffs. Flying low, just over our heads, the puffins were particularly curious – and curious looking. Black and white with bright orange-red bills, they looked like flying penguins.

From the sea we could see several caves in the rocky shore. Scott and I decided to explore one in our kayak.

Scott and I paddled past Uliaga on our first clear day. The blue skies made it easy to forget all the days of rain and fog. We felt as though we were kayaking through our own private paradise.

Puffins, with their exaggerated features, look a bit like clowns. They provided a friendly greeting on almost every island. I'm sure they were as curious about the "invaders" in the yellow and red boats as we were about them.

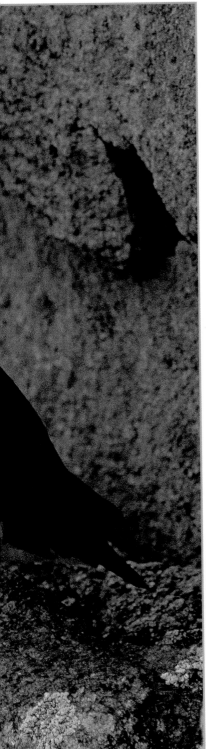

It was dark and spooky, and we could hear water lapping onto a beach deep inside. Just as my eyes were adjusting to the darkness, something collided with my head, knocking my cap into the water. For a minute I thought some Aleut ghost was throwing rocks at us!

Scott laughed and pointed to a puffin that was flapping its wings furiously as it flew out into the bright sunlight. The bird had been sleeping on a rocky perch when we surprised it. Puffins are not particularly graceful flyers, and when this one took off, it dropped down low and hit my head. As I picked up my floating hat, I wondered who was more startled – the bird or me.

We were constantly in awe of the grand size of the island walls we paddled past. Here, the volcanic cliffs of Kagamil rise straight up from the sea, dwarfing our tiny kayak.

June 19: The Village Where It Is Always Warm

We made camp on a cliff high above the rocky shore at the south end of Kagamil. I named it Eagle Camp, because when we arrived we were greeted by two large bald eagles – mom and dad – that were taking care of a pair of newborn chicks in a nest above the beach.

This afternoon we hiked through the tall grass, up hills leading to the island's volcano. We climbed above the fog, gaining incredible views of the sea and the other islands. Every step we took, we thought about what it must have been like for the Aleuts who lived here until 150 years ago. Sometimes it felt as if one of them was walking right next to us, guiding us up and down the hills to the most beautiful spots and the best views.

Thousands of years ago when the Aleuts arrived here, they found the sea filled with fish, sea otters, sea lions, and whales. They depended on the ocean for their food and clothing. While the men spent long days at sea hunting

Broad meadows strewn with boulders (left) cover the interiors of some islands. Now grass-covered, these rocks were probably tossed from an exploding volcano. Aleuts built their houses closer to the beach. From there they could easily launch their kayaks when it was time to hunt seals and sea lions (right).

and fishing in their kayaks, the women made clothes
from the skins of seals and wove baskets from grass.

At one time as many as 150 Aleuts lived on Kagamil.
They called the place where we hiked today the Village
Where It Is Always Warm. It was easy to understand why
the Aleuts chose this place to live. Hot air rising out of volcanic
vents heats the ground. When Sean stuck his hand in the
steam, he pulled it back fast, surprised by how hot it was.

The Aleuts also built their homes near small ponds and

*Scott and Sean take a closer look at steam rising from holes
in the earth near the Village Where It Is Always Warm.
Heat from the island's volcano helped preserve mummies
that the Aleuts buried in caves along cliffs such as these.*

streams, where they could get water for cooking and drinking. To protect themselves from the wind, they dug their houses into the ground and covered them with roofs made from driftwood and grass. Many families lived together in one long house – grandfathers, grandmothers, fathers, mothers, children, aunts and uncles – as many as 40 people. For light they burned seal and whale fat in lamps.

Standing at the edge of a cliff that dropped steeply to the sea, we could see steam pouring out of small caves near the water. It was in those hard-to-reach caves that archaeologists discovered Aleut mummies more than a hundred years ago. The mummies were buried with their kayaks, clothing, food, and grass bags. The Aleuts were smart. They knew that heat from the volcano would help preserve the mummies. Today there are no mummies in the caves. They have all been moved to museums in Russia and the United States.

Even though we know the Aleuts are long gone, we often feel we are not alone. I frequently find myself looking back over my shoulder, thinking I will catch sight of someone walking behind us, looking out for us.

Underground houses were entered by ladder through one or two hatches in the roof. Hanging grass mats created "rooms" off the main living area and provided some privacy for the people living there.

June 20: Flying Rocks and Rotten Eggs

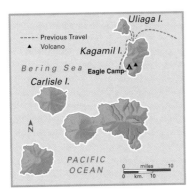

Early this morning we tried to climb to the top of Kagamil's sleeping volcano.

It was almost snowing as we climbed straight up through the thick, slippery grass. When we got to the loose dirt and rock that covered the top half of the mountain, the fog was so thick we could barely see one another. Strong winds blowing from the top nearly knocked us backward. Scott, with his bright colored jacket, stayed out in front, leading us like a beacon up the hill.

I was standing next to Barry near the top of the 3,000-foot volcano when a loose rock flew by, just missing us. It was the size of a softball and moving as fast as 60 miles an hour. It could have knocked one of us to the bottom of the mountain. "That was lucky!" Barry said. I could see he was not smiling.

The four of us sat down on the loose rock to talk about the dangers of continuing. We were 400 feet from the top and felt as though we had stepped onto another planet. White smoke that smelled like rotten eggs puffed out of deep holes on the mountainside. Because of the thick fog, we couldn't see where we were going. We knew if one of us were to slip and fall and break a bone, it could take days for help to reach us – *if* we could raise someone over the radio. When we made the decision to turn around, we were all relieved. As more loose rocks whizzed by, we headed down to the soft grass of the fields below.

Our first chance to climb a volcano came on Kagamil. Heat from the volcano had melted most of the snow on its slopes, but loose rocks and thick fog made our ascent difficult. Here, Sean and I pause to study the mountain, looking for a safe route to the top.

Day 9

June 21: Crossing to Chuginadak

As Scott and I took down our tent this morning I spotted Sean sitting on the rocky beach below, a map unfolded on his knees. He was holding a compass and the GPS, a computerized navigation system that uses satellites orbiting Earth to plot exact locations.

He was carefully marking out a route between Kagamil and Chuginadak. It would be our most exposed crossing so far. As team navigator, he wanted to make sure we followed the most direct route possible.

About eleven o'clock we pushed our kayaks into the ocean, one after the other. The fog was thick, and we were very concerned about becoming separated. We talked about how important it was to stick close together. If one boat had trouble during the crossing, the other kayak would be close by.

Within just ten minutes the fog swallowed Kagamil behind us. Chuginadak was buried somewhere in the fog ahead of us. It was frightening to be in a small kayak on such rough water and not be able to see any sign of land. Never before had I felt so alone. For all I knew the wind could be blowing us far off course, carrying us out to sea.

I tried to imagine how the Aleuts managed in conditions like these. How had they found their way in the fog? We had sophisticated navigation tools; they had only their instincts and the stars. With every paddle stroke, I thought about what it must have been like for them in their simple kayaks and clothing made from the intestines of seals.

The Aleuts depended on the sea for everything and were incredible hunters. They used harpoons and wooden clubs to hunt seals, otters, and whales, and handmade hooks to catch fish that could weigh more than 100 pounds. Imagine the skill required to kill a 20-ton whale from a kayak! A successful hunt was a big event, since a whale could feed everyone in the village for several months.

Everything the Aleuts needed to survive – food, clothing, and shelter – they got from the sea. Killing a whale was a huge event. Hooks (top left) strong enough to catch fish weighing a hundred pounds or more were carved from whalebone. Whale teeth often decorated hunting hats made from driftwood (right).

"Paddle for your life" became our motto as we crossed from island to island, battling strong winds and cold water. Spectacular views, such as this waterfall near Skiff Cove on Chuginadak (right), helped make all the danger and hard work worthwhile.

These seas were big. Plus we had to deal with swirls and rip tides. Scott and I followed close behind Sean and Barry's red-topped kayak. They zigzagged back and forth, pushed by the wind and currents, trying to follow the compass mounted in front of Sean. Waves washed over the boats as we paddled, and we had to shout to each other in order to be heard above the roar of the wind.

"Paddle harder on your right side," Scott yelled to me from the back of the boat. We were trying to pull alongside Sean and Barry, who were nearly swallowed up in the fog.

"Keep your eye on them," Scott yelled. "We don't want to lose them." While he kept his eye on the waves and the wind coming at us from the side and from behind, I focused on keeping Sean and Barry in sight.

After two hours of nonstop paddling, we finally made out the dim outline of Chuginadak, the biggest of the Islands of Four Mountains. Sean had picked a 150-foot-tall waterfall as our target, and there it was, straight ahead. It made for a beautiful welcome to the island the Aleuts call the birthplace of their people.

Day 10

June 22: The Day the Wind Stopped

The wind stopped blowing at exactly 6:43 p.m.

Since Day One, when we took our first steps onto Kagamil, the wind has blown. Sometimes just a breeze, other times strong enough to knock down our tents and carry off anything we have not tied or weighted down.

Now, for the first time in nearly two weeks, we can hear birds singing and waves breaking calmly on the beach. Surprised by the sudden change, we crawled out of our tents, took off our stocking caps, and unzipped our jackets. What was going on? we wondered. The Birthplace of the Winds didn't feel right without at least a small breeze.

While we cook our pasta and tomato sauce – outside, under a teal-colored sky – we talk in normal voices, no longer having to shout. Where has the wind gone? When will it return?

A wall of driftwood breaks the wind as Scott and I take time out to write in our journals. We tried to do this daily so we wouldn't forget the details of any events. As navigator, Sean (right) spent much of his camp time figuring out our next route. A computerized device called a GPS was invaluable in plotting a course among the islands.

The wind is back – fierce and furious, so loud it woke us up in the middle of the night. Our tent vibrated as the wind hit it with the punch of a heavyweight boxer. I reached out of my sleeping bag and pushed against the ceiling with both hands, doing what I could to keep the tent from being blown over.

With the wind came a hard, cold rain. The combination meant we had to spend all day inside our tents, doing the only things you can do inside a tent: eat, sleep, talk, read; eat, sleep, talk, read. Luckily we had anticipated many days like this and had brought 20 books – mysteries, novels, adventures, classics. Our two-man tents are perfectly comfortable as long as we are lying down. Sitting up is difficult, because our heads rub against the low ceilings. We cook and eat sitting cross-legged and slightly bent over.

A few times during the day we had to get outside, to stretch and breathe some fresh air. Going out required putting on rain jackets, rain pants, hats, gloves, and boots. The wind was blowing 40 miles an hour. It drove the rain into us like sharp needles and forced the waterfalls cascading over the tall cliffs around our camp to flow sideways and uphill. This is *real* Aleutian weather!

On the days when we were stuck inside our tents – rainstorms
raging outside, winds howling – we were glad we had thought
to bring along some books to keep us entertained. Here Scott and
I share a laugh from one of them, while Sean (left) cooks up a big
pan of rice and curry for his and Barry's dinner.

Day 12

June 24: Sean's Discovery

Near the end of our second full day of being tent-bound, Sean called for Barry to get his camera gear then banged on our tent, pleading with us to come out. He was excited about something. Pulling on rain pants and jackets, Scott and I scrambled out.

"You'll never guess what I found," he shouted excitedly over the wind. "Up there, over the hill." Apparently he'd gone stir-crazy inside his tent and had decided to take a hike up the hills of Chuginadak. That's where he made his discovery.

"Come on, let's go," he shouted over the wind. "Follow me." Curious, and trusting that his excitement must be about something special, we climbed the steep hills and crossed fast-moving streams, straining against the wind. After 45 minutes we reached the top of the last hill, where Sean pointed to a silver shape. From a distance it looked like a big, white whale lying in the green grass. But as we got closer, we could see it was a small silver airplane.

In the 1940s, during World War II, there was fighting in the Aleutian Islands between the armies of Japan and the United States. Hundreds of men died on the bigger islands (many from the cold weather, rather than at the hands of enemy soldiers). This two-person U.S. Navy plane must have been shot down and crashed here on Chuginadak. We inspected the upside-down plane for an hour, wondering about the men who had flown it and what might have happened to them. There were bullet holes in the side of the plane but no skeletons. Had the men parachuted out of the plane before it crashed? If so, where had they ended up? On land or in the middle of the cold ocean? Had they lived or died? I wrote down the plane's serial number so that I can try to find out what happened when I get back home.

Our excitement at finding the remains of a World War II plane made us temporarily forget the bad weather. We crawled underneath the plane to get a better look at the interior. Seat belts were unhooked, the glass in the gauges was intact, and rubber moldings were in perfect condition more than 50 years after the plane had crashed. The engine, a propeller, and a small bomb that had never exploded lay off to the side. We searched all around, but found no clues to explain what might have happened to the pilot or the gunner.

June 26: Applegate Cove

Uliaga I.

— Travel
- - - Previous Travel
▲ Volcano

Kagamil I.

Bering Sea

Carlisle I. Applegate
Cove

Skiff Cove
Camp

Carlisle Camp ▲

Applegate Cove
Camp

N

Carlisle Pass

▲ Mt. Cleveland

Chuginadak I.

PACIFIC
OCEAN

0 miles 10

0 km. 10

We left Skiff Cove yesterday, after the 60-hour storm finally ended, and paddled along the northern shore of Chuginadak to Applegate Cove. Near the entrance to the cove stood 6,000-foot-tall, snow-covered Mount Cleveland. It was the middle of the afternoon when we pulled our kayaks onto the black sand beach. A cold drizzle was falling.

After setting up camp in a sheltered area of the four-mile-long beach, I went exploring. The beach was littered with dozens of plastic bottles, pails and boxes, life buoys and ropes –

most of it from Russian, Japanese, and American fishing boats. Some of the things – big logs, for example – had been carried from thousands of miles away by ocean currents.

Today was bright and sunny, so we were tempted to try to climb Mount Cleveland, one of the biggest challenges of our trip. But with the weather in our favor, we opted to try to paddle across to Carlisle instead.

Since we know that we will be returning to Applegate Cove

This sign from a Japanese fishing boat was just part of the trash we found washed up on the driftwood-strewn beach at Applegate Cove. Roughly translated, it says, "Watch Your Step." Our camp was on a sandy beach in a site protected from the wind. The smaller of Chuginadak's two volcanoes towered some 3,000 feet above it.

to meet the *Miss Peppers* in 11 days, we decided to stash some of our food in waterproof bags under a rock ledge at the campsite. We were surprised to discover that we are running a bit short. We will be OK as long as the weather stays good, but if the big rains and winds return and the *Miss Peppers* is delayed, we might be in trouble.

"I'm going to start keeping my share of food in my sleeping bag at night," joked Sean. We laughed because he shares his tent with Barry, who likes to eat five or six times a day.

We left for Carlisle late in the afternoon. This far north we still had seven or eight hours of daylight. It was a long paddle, but wind conditions were in our favor. Two hours later, we reached the calm waters off our fourth island.

Here we face a new problem: no fresh water. We had assumed that snowmelt from Carlisle's volcano would create streams or pools, but the creeks and gullies are completely dry. Luckily each of us brought a big bag of fresh water from our camp at Applegate Cove, but our stay on Carlisle will have to be brief.

Hoods up and rubber gloves on, we headed for Carlisle Island (left). On cold days like this there was no time to stop for a drink of water or even to wipe your nose. Fortunately, the cold didn't keep wildflowers like these Nootka lupines from blooming. They were always a welcome sight.

We were out of our tents before 6 a.m. to get a jump on kayaking all the way from Carlisle to Herbert. We wanted to catch a ride on the strong, early morning outgoing tide. As we packed up our gear, I measured the air temperature. During the night it had dropped below freezing, and by 6 it was still only 34 degrees and snowing. I didn't even want to think about what would happen if a kayak tipped over today.

"Maybe we should have stayed in our sleeping bags this morning," muttered Scott as we sealed the hatches on our kayak and pushed off from the rocky shore. A family of seals popped their heads up through the seaweed to watch us leave.

Once free of the seaweed, we were in for a very fast ride. In the middle of Chuginadak Pass we began to plow into five-foot waves that washed over our boats and sent a cold spray down the insides of our jackets. The strong tides pulled us into an even stronger current, whipping us through the waves as though we'd been shot from slingshots. We were dangerously out of control, but it was too late to turn around.

Our paddling took on a new urgency as we looked for a landmark to aim for on Herbert. "Pick anything," Scott shouted to Barry, who was steering the lead kayak.

The hardest part of leaving an island in rough weather was getting through the heavy surf that pounded onto the beach. Sitting up front, I usually got hit harder than Scott. A fierce wave had ripped off my hat and goggles just minutes before Barry took this picture.

Being greeted by a group of sea lions at Herbert Island was a highlight of our trip. Hundreds of thousands of sea lions lived in the Aleutians before fur traders greatly reduced their numbers. Today they compete with fishermen for food.

"What about that *V* in the hills, the dark spot between the two meadows?" Barry yelled back over the wind.

After two hours of cold, tiring paddling, we reached Herbert – the fifth and last of the Islands of Four Mountains. We were greeted with barks of hello from some sea lions perched on a rock like a welcoming committee.

We made camp on a grassy cliff high above the sea. There are several ponds nearby, so we have plenty of fresh water. Our plan for the next four days is to explore the island and kayak along its coastline. Herbert's volcano turns out to have a very odd shape. Thousands of years ago it blew its top, leaving behind a jagged peak that is a thousand feet higher on one side than the other.

Streams formed from melting snow provided plenty of fresh water for drinking on the first three islands we visited. Our stay on Carlisle was short lived because we found no water. On Herbert we had to get our water from ponds, as Sean is doing here. Since there was nothing around to contaminate it, we felt safe drinking it.

Day 17

June 29: Full Moon Camp

Just after midnight, a strong light flashed through our tent walls. Was it possible somebody else had arrived on Herbert? We stumbled out of our tents to take a look. No one was there. The light was coming from something else we hadn't seen since we arrived: a full moon. It was a good sign. June 29 would be sunny and blue – a perfect present for my birthday.

In the middle of the day I celebrated by taking a bath in the seaweed-strewn, 35-degree salt water of the cove near our camp. I couldn't do much more than dunk myself, but it was still a real treat. I dried off, put on nearly clean clothes, and sat for a long time on the sun-warmed rocks looking at Mount Cleveland

We tried to bathe at least once a week. On Herbert I used my dinner bowl to take a "bowl bath" on my birthday. The water was freezing cold and full of seaweed, but it felt good to be clean.

across the pass. The white smoke spiraling from its peak stood out against the deep blue of the sky. The volcano looked impressive, daunting. I'm worried that it might be too difficult to climb or that bad weather will keep us from even trying.

Just before dinner I announced that I had a small surprise: Several cans of sardines – something different in honor of my birthday. It was a welcome change and the perfect appetizer for a meal of freeze-dried beef stew. This birthday was definitely one I'll never forget.

June 30: The Hunting Cabin

This afternoon was sunny, so we paddled to the north end of Herbert and pulled our kayaks onto a beach of round rocks. Climbing uphill through waist-high grass, we discovered a field that was protected from the wind. In its center we found the ruins of a hunting cabin. Its roof had caved in, and its walls had fallen down. In the rubble we found broken pieces of an old teacup and a silver knife.

In the mid-1800s, Russian hunters brought foxes to these islands and raised them for their fur. There were no predators to eat the foxes, so the animals flourished. Their pelts were sold in Russia, where there was a great demand for warm hats and coats. Now, the hunters and the foxes – like the Aleuts – are long gone.

July 2: Return to Applegate

Uliaga I.

— Travel
- - - Previous Travel
▲ Volcano

Bering Sea

Kagamil I.

Carlisle I.

▲ Applegate Cove Camp

N

▲ Mt. Cleveland

Chuginadak I.

Herbert Camp ▲ Herbert I.

PACIFIC OCEAN

0 miles 10
0 km. 10

"Keep paddling! Hard!" Scott yelled from the back of the boat. I barely heard his words. The wind was blowing forcefully, and the currents were much faster than we had expected. It was almost snowing, and big, cold waves crashed over our kayak. We were halfway between Herbert and Chuginadak. As I plunged my paddle into the black sea, the thought kept running through my head that perhaps we should have spent one more day on Herbert.

We were exhausted and our feet were freezing, but we had made it safely back to Chuginadak. Scott and I unloaded our boat for the last time, then Sean helped us carry it closer to camp. It felt good to be back on the familiar black sands of Applegate Cove.

The constant paddling made my arms feel like hundred-pound weights hanging from my shoulders. Just when I felt we'd made it through the hardest part of the crossing, a fierce wind blowing down from the top of Mount Cleveland hit us right in the face. I couldn't image worse conditions.

We were headed back to Applegate Cove. As we entered the pass separating Chuginadak and Carlisle, the sun came out, the wind died a little, and we felt as though we were on easy street. That's when it hit – the strongest wind we had experienced in almost a month of paddling. Blowing from the south, off the Pacific Ocean, it raced right at us through a narrow slot that nearly divides Chuginadak in two. It almost stopped our boat in its place.

We were still four miles from camp. Waves broke across the bow. With each I swallowed frigid seawater. Every stroke of my paddle threw a cold spray of water into Scott's face. After an hour of struggling, we finally reached the shallows. Jumping out of the kayak, we pulled it onto the black sand beach. Sean and Barry pulled in just minutes behind us. It was our last crossing and, although we could barely stand, we celebrated with a long drink of *fresh* water.

July 4: Climbing Mount Cleveland

Uliaga I.

- - - - - Previous Travel
▲ Volcano

Kagamil I.

Bering Sea

Carlisle I.

▲ Applegate Cove Camp

▲ Mt. Cleveland

Chuginadak I.

Herbert I.

PACIFIC OCEAN

0 miles 10
0 km. 10

N

It is the Fourth of July – Independence Day. Since we are far from parades and fireworks, we decided to celebrate the day by climbing Mount Cleveland. The sun is bright and the sky is clear, the most beautiful day we've seen since arriving.

Yesterday we studied the mountain from our camp, trying to decide which route to the summit would be the best. Should we march straight up or zigzag from side to side through what we knew was deep, soft snow? Should we go around to the other side and look for an easier, less steep route? From where we sat it looked very dangerous, maybe even impossible. We decided to take the zigzag route even though it meant hiking through more snow.

"How long do you think it will take?" I asked Sean.

"About 15 hours round-trip – *if* we're lucky."

To get to the mountain we first had to walk across the four-mile-long beach and then hike two miles over grassy hills and up the exposed layers of sharp, black lava rock. We finally reached the edge of the snow, halfway up the mountain, two hours later. We sat on the rocks and attached crampons to our boots. The sharp spikes would

Climbing above the clouds on our way to the top of Mount Cleveland, we were rewarded with this magnificent view of Carlisle Island. Standing more than a mile above the sea, we could also see the other islands in the group and the routes we had kayaked among them.

help keep us from slipping on the ice and snow. We put on harnesses in case we had to hook ourselves together with a rope for safety and used our ice axes for balance.

We climbed single file through the deep, wet snow, zigzagging from side to side, slowly, carefully, one footstep at a time. The most difficult part was keeping our balance. A fall would mean sliding more than 2,000 feet to the rocks below.

The higher we climbed, the clearer the sky became. Uliaga and Kagamil jumped out of the blue sea in the distance. We could easily make out bays where we had landed and made camps as we paddled among the islands. Barry and I went to the edge of the mountain and looked over. There, directly in front of us, was Carlisle – the perfect photograph.

The wind was so strong that we were forced to crawl the final 50 feet on our hands and knees. When we finally stood up, the volcano's giant, smoking crater was right in front of us. Beyond, we could see the fifth island – Herbert – with its blown-off volcano.

It took us nearly eight hours of nonstop climbing to reach the summit, but it was worth it. From the top of Mount Cleveland we could see all of the Islands of Four Mountains, a truly special view on a very special day.

The wind was blowing 60 miles an hour, and the sulfur stench from the volcano was awful, but nothing could keep us from smiling. We were standing on top of Mount Cleveland – highest peak in the Islands of Four Mountains. Even Barry managed to get in the picture. We enjoyed the view from the top for about half an hour, then began the six-hour hike back to camp. It was a Fourth of July we will always remember.

July 7: The Return of the Miss Peppers

We were awakened by the *putt-putt-putt* of a motor. Jumping out of our tents we saw the *Miss Peppers* coming out of the fog. We had picked this date a month before and had told Captain Don Graves to pick us up at Applegate Cove. Sure enough, he arrived on the exact date. We were happy and a little surprised to see him. We had expected him to be at least one day late, maybe even a week because of bad weather and huge seas. He greeted us with a big smile, obviously relieved to find all of us here and in one piece.

"So . . . what's new?" he asked, laughing.

It took several trips to transfer all of our gear to the *Miss Peppers*. Two hours later, we pulled away from Chuginadak. It felt very different to see the island from the comfort of a big fishing boat instead of from the cockpits of our small kayaks.

Before Captain Don put the *Miss Peppers* into high gear for the trip back to Dutch Harbor and civilization, we asked him to go slow so we could have one last look at the islands we now know so well. We are not quite ready to leave. Despite the rain, the fog, the winds, the cold ocean, the hard paddles, and the difficult climbs, we feel strangely sad. We will miss the daily challenges, the camaraderie, and the simple way of life. Most of all, we will miss the incomparable beauty we have found on these remote islands.

Sunset turns the top of Mount Cleveland – and the smoke swirling from its volcano – pink. Our kayaks rest peacefully on the black sand of Applegate Cove, ready to be loaded onto the Miss Peppers *for the trip back to Dutch Harbor.*

Afterword

One month later we were back at our homes in California and New York, enjoying *real* summer weather. Sean is working in his law office and learning to fly in his spare time. Scott is selling outdoor clothing and equipment when he's not kayaking the big surf off California. And Barry and I are busy planning another kayak trip – this time to Vietnam.

We each have a lifetime of memories from our Aleutian adventure. We achieved our goals of exploring all five of the Islands of Four Mountains and climbing their volcanoes, fortunately without injury.

Remember the plane we found on Chuginadak? The Department of Defense sent two researchers to the island – aboard the *Miss Peppers* – to investigate. Unfortunately, fog and rain kept them from finding the plane, so its story remains a mystery.

Wherever future adventures take me, I will carry in my memory images of the Islands of Four Mountains: the feel of the black sand beaches; the smell of wet grass; the cold, strong winds; waiting inside our orange tents for the storms to stop; paddling hard for hour after hour in rough water, surrounded by fog; the sound of a puffin's wings flapping as it flies low over my head; and the sight of snow-capped volcanoes rising out of the Bering Sea, surrounded by wide blue skies and big white clouds. They are beautiful images of one of the most magical and mysterious corners of the world.

It is this kind of image – soft buttercups framing calm, deep-blue water and Mount Cleveland's towering, snow-covered volcano – that stays in my head many months after returning home from the Islands of Four Mountains.

*All images by
Barry Tessman except:*

13 up, Lithograph from drawing by Friedrich H. von Kittlitz, in the atlas to Lütke's *Voyage*, 1835, courtesy Beinecke Library, Yale University; 18, Engraving from the atlas to Lisiansky's *Putesh-estvie*, 1812, courtesy Beinecke Library, Yale University; 26–27, Jeffrey O. Foott; 29, Courtesy Beinecke Library, Yale University; 31, Arctic Studies Center, Smithsonian Institution; 34 up, from *Archaeological Investigations in the Aleutian Islands*, by Waldemar Jochelson, published by the Carnegie Institution of Washington, 1925; 34 lo, "An Arctic Province: Alaska and the Seal Islands" by Henry W. Elliott. London: Sampson Low, Marston, Searle & Rivington, 1886. University of British Columbia Library, special Collections and University Archives Division; 35, "A Man of Oonalashka," drawn by John Webber (pl. 48 in Cook's Atlas, 1784), published in *Aleut and Eskimo Art: Tradition and Innovation in South Alaska*, by Dorothy Jean Ray, published by University of Washington Press, Seattle; 50–51, Ron E. Lauber

Grateful thanks to George Dyson's *Baidarka: The Kayak*, (Alaska Northwest Books, 1986), for illustrations and inspiration.

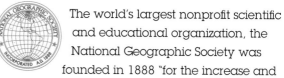

The world's largest nonprofit scientific and educational organization, the National Geographic Society was founded in 1888 "for the increase and diffusion of geographic knowledge." Since then it has supported scientific exploration and spread information to its more than nine million members worldwide.

The National Geographic Society educates and inspires millions every day through magazines, books, television programs, videos, maps and atlases, research grants, the National Geographic Bee, teacher workshops, and innovative classroom materials.

The Society is supported through membership dues and income from the sale of its educational products. Members receive NATIONAL GEOGRAPHIC magazine — the Society's official journal — discounts on Society products, and other benefits.

For more information about the National Geographic Society and its educational programs and publications, please call 1-800-NGS-LINE (647-5463), or write to the following address:

National Geographic Society
1145 17th Street N.W.
Washington, D.C. 20036-4688 U.S.A.

Visit the Society's Web site at
www.nationalgeographic.com.